I0462337

The Right to Self-Determination

By Lord Loveday Ememe and available from Lulu and Amazon

The Constitution and policing

Heresy

Starfleet

The Supernatural

Creation

Deterrence

Stalking

The Media

Adam

Criminal Responsibility

The Wicked

Common Law

Racism

Regulation

Science

ISBN: 978-0-244-62180-3

Table of Contents

The rule of law

What is the rule of law?

The rule of law is the creation of a civilization, the state, to cater to the needs of man. These needs include security from all types of danger. The civilization's primary objective is the protection of man from practices or things or beings that threaten the security of man. Man is defined by international and domestic legislations, the bible, and common law, as a living being without supernatural powers and senses. This definition is important in identifying the being or beings amongst other beings that is the ruler or standard for defining or identifying a threat or danger.

The delicate nature of man that requires civility from things, practices, and beings in order not to breach or threaten the security of man, in order not to harm man mentally or physically, make man the law in living form.

The establishment of the rule of law, which is the creation of a properly constituted police service, is a one off process if done correctly, legally. If done incorrectly as is the case at present, a political police service, it will facilitate the opposite effect on the law, the civil noble lord, it becomes a weapon used to destabilize or disrupt or destroy.

The existence of the civil noble scientific constitution, civil beings, beings without supernatural powers and senses, confirms the existence of the real rule of law. The real rule of law is being challenged or undermined by supernatural beings unlawfully pretending to be civil beings with the introduction or imposition of the political rule of law. The political rule of law is lawlessness, in the forms of religions, democracy, homosexuality, paedophilia, racism, the persecution of civil beings, the slaughter and abuse of animals, advocacy of the supremacy of supernatural beings, flesh-eating carnivores, inequality, poverty, etcetera.

The greatest threat to the civil constitution is the supernatural constitution, confirming that the purpose of the rule of law, the police service, is to regulate supernatural beings.

The political rule of law is another way of saying that there is no right to self-determination, everyone eligible is at the mercy of another, the unregulated interest from another. The eligibility for the political role play, responsible for the political rule of law, is the supernatural political constitution. Participation requires supernatural powers and senses. The legal principle, criminal responsibility, applies only to those capable of participating in the supernatural political role plays, supernatural beings. Civil beings, the victims, are ineligible to participate in these role plays. Civil beings are not of political constitutions but are of legal constitutions. These are some of the words used for the delivery of goods services indicating that the purpose of the rule of law, the police service, is to regulate supernatural beings. The words are capital or capitalism, budget, economy or economics, science, etcetera. These are regulatory jargons to control supernaturalism for health and safety purposes and not to introduce poverty. They are used to introduce orderliness and not disorder or clutter to the delivery of goods and services. These words or concepts are regulatory, meant to represent the conversion of the supernatural to the scientific. Under this political lawless rule of law there are two types of supernaturalisms practiced by supernatural beings, the direct supernaturalism, and the indirect supernaturalism.

The direct supernaturalism is the practice of supernatural beings stalking the vulnerable especially civil beings supernaturally as gods of civil beings evidenced in their interpretation and application of the Christian teachings in the forms of churches, synagogues, mosques, etcetera.

The indirect supernaturalism is the red or demonic use of regulatory jargons like capitalism, economy, or economics, linked to the market economy, the stock market, giving supernatural beings an unfair advantage over civil beings establishing inequality and the supremacy of supernatural beings.

Supernatural children must be educated on how to be law abiding supernatural beings and not deceived into being criminalized by pretending to be of civil constitutions and neglecting their obligations to the state as supernatural beings. They are deceived or manipulated into lawlessness and initiated into the red colonization of the world, the political rule of law. Civil beings have already paid their taxes; supernatural beings have to fulfil their obligations to the state, a type of taxation.

Given the population and the nature of the supernatural constitution, there has to be the rule of law, a permanent police service. This police service will be the only employment charged with maintaining peace and security and the provision of goods and services to everyone. The police service will dismantle all the nonsense created by the red colonization of the planet, making people work unnecessarily. The police service will dismantle all of the insane pointless problems they deliberately created in the world to create activities for themselves at the expense of peace and security.

Unfortunately, all public offices under the current political rule of law that have plagued this planet for millennia are tainted with demonism. They are responsible for deaths, diseases, ageing, poverty, inequality, the unlawful persecution of civil beings, etcetera. These public offices or public officials are not honourable; they are undermining the sacredness of the real rule of law.

The real rule of law is a state service, a police service, and privatization under this rule of law is an attempt to secede and will be considered an act of treason. The right to self – determination or privatization, attempts to secede; under the state service will be a criminal offence, a political revolution.

The political rule of law is lawlessness or organized barbarism that uses governance through public offices or a public office to establish and maintain a constant state of anarchy. Anarchy or hostile conditions cater to the hostile nature of the demon, supernatural beings are susceptible to hostile conditions, are corruptible, the weak link in the establishment of the real rule of law, hence the expression, selling your soul to the devil.

The real rule of law ensures that civil rights are applied correctly and not manipulated for political purposes. An example is the civil right to life. The right to life means indefinite lifespan or immortality, the elimination of all diseases or illnesses, the elimination of poverty, and the security of person from supernatural attacks.

All the supernatural political lawless manifestoes of political parties around the world cannot compete with the legal manifesto of the real rule of law.

As a consequence of the adverse effects of the political rule of law on the mental and physical health of civil beings, the political rule of law is a declaration of war on the legal rule of law.

The real rule of law operates within the parameters of the reality of possibility given the existence of the civil and supernatural constitutions, unlike the political rule of law that operates outside reality, delusional.

The political rule of law is an attempt to secede from the legal rule of law by supernatural beings. The severe punishment for attempts at secession is as a consequence of the sacred determination of its impossibility.

Under the real rule of law, traditional rulers or legal rulers are civil beings, without supernatural powers and senses that are born or created to rule. These rulers are the modern commissioners of the civilization or metropolitan police service. The word traditional that is used to refer to legal rulers is in honour of the first legal ruler under the real rule of law, Lord Adam.

Variants of the legal rule of law, political manifestoes of the political rule of law, are possible because of the wicked nature of the supernatural constitution. Hostile conditions do not have the same effect on supernatural beings as they do on civil beings. Supernatural beings as a consequence could create hell on earth without realizing it.

Civil beings are exempt from supernatural political role plays under the political rule of law by common law, international and domestic legislations. This has been achieved by not acknowledging the existence of the supernatural constitution. This is not significant when supernatural beings interact with each other under these legislations but extremely significant when a civil being is involved. Under these circumstances when civil beings are involved in order not to commit a crime or crimes impersonating a civil being or civil beings, they have to regard the communications of real civil beings as instructions or commands or orders.

The real rule of law requires legal relationships with civil beings and not political relationships as if supernatural beings are gods to civil beings rather than submission to civil beings as rulers of supernatural beings. The word ruler is not an oppressive word as the political rule of law has made it appear to be, under the real rule of law it can be referred to as standard or guide or peace or determinant or commissioner etcetera. The ruler is a being of a constitution that can be applied universally as the standard for health and safety purposes for the provision of goods and services, including the provision of security.

Unfortunately, under the political rule of law interaction or association or relationships are hostile, based on deception and lies that encourage fighting. It ensures the loss of self-respect or dignity; as a consequence it is dishonourable to be party to any government operating under the political rule of law.

The supernatural constitution is not legal, it is a political constitution, all governments headed by a supernatural being whether a military regime or a monarchy or a civilian regime are variants of the legal rule of law, as a consequence operating under the political rule of law.

The political rule of law is lawlessness. How do you define crime under the political rule of law? How do you fight corruption within corruption? It is like being worried about a rat in your house, rat infestation, when your house is on fire. The serious problem civil beings have under the political rule of law, is the attempt by supernatural beings to define good and evil within corruption, they try to fit civil beings into their definition of good by force. Unfortunately, their definition of good within lawlessness is also evil. Civil beings are good naturally, and naturally establish the real rule of law that defines good and evil.

Under the real rule of law, which is a properly constituted police service, supernatural beings have obligations to the state, a type of taxation, for the development and security of the state best achieved with similar principles used in the Nigerian youth service corps, a compulsory national service for graduates. In this case it will be permanent but rotational.

Role play is the fuel for the political rule of law, supernatural beings lying about their real constitutions and pretending to be civil beings neglecting their obligations to the state. There is a difference between lying about your constitution and the restriction of the use of supernatural powers and senses to be law abiding. If supernatural beings are interested in acting they can have careers in the movie industry. There has to be a distinction between fiction and reality, the real world. The whole world cannot be a movie set to cater to the nature of the supernatural constitution at the expense of peace and security.

Unfortunately, within the demonic application and interpretation of the Christian teachings there is a n between different groups of supernatural beings referred to as red demons and blue angels.

The reds are supernatural beings that advocate the supremacy of supernatural beings over civil beings, responsible for lawlessness, poverty, inequality, death, diseases, ageing, etcetera. They favour living conditions or processes that are hostile to beings that are not supernatural beings, like the vulnerable civil beings. Examples of these are religions, red economics or red capitalism, politics or democracy or the political rule of law, the red version, or interpretation of the Christian teachings, red healthcare system, etcetera.

The blues are meant to be law abiding supernatural beings that advocate the supremacy of the civil constitution. They are traditionalists or legalists or lawyers that use the civil constitution as the standard for the provision of goods and services ensuring that the health and safety standard is universal for the purpose of peace and security for everyone. Unfortunately, the red colonization of the world, the corruption of supernatural beings, has made it almost impossible to establish the real rule of law.

Law abiding supernatural beings cannot be associated with any type of fighting, in order not to be corrupt and as a consequence under the control of the reds.

Political processes or methods are types of fighting, the truth by the identification and distinction of civil beings as rulers with entitlements that are the correct application of civil rights is the legal way to establish the real rule of law, a nonfighting or non-political method of establishing the real rule of law.

The sacred determination has been made regarding the achievement of the real rule of law; the criteria for establishing a properly constituted police service require civil beings to be the commissioners of the police service. The civil being or beings must have all the rights and privileges of a ruler, these rights and privileges although currently being abused by supernatural beings pretending to be rulers are sacred disability rights for civil beings given the differences between the civil and supernatural constitutions. If supernatural beings try to undermine the role or authority of civil beings by using or manipulating civil beings as if puppets they will be creating a political faction that will be challenged by other political factions.

The supernatural constitution is political, the political is hostile or fighting or revolutionary, revolution against an established order or standard. In order for supernatural beings to operate legally, they need to get their legal status or legality by operating under the authority of the civil constitution as leader or ruler.

Reds need to corrupt supernatural beings by luring them away from being law abiding, any form of the political or fighting gets them under the dominance or control or colonization of the reds. So, supernatural beings that consider themselves blues are manipulated or goaded into political methods or processes, to directly or indirectly undermine or compromise the authority of civil beings as rulers enabling their corruption and colonization by the reds. In order not to be corrupt supernatural beings have to avoid the political and embrace the legal, they need to be truthful without being supernatural or political. The truth requires the scientific process with the commission of civil beings as rulers.

The truth cannot be defeated or opposed regardless of the number of reds. This is why the reds always favour the democratic political method supported by role plays that hide their identities. Role plays are lies that hide the truth, creating the necessary breeding ground for demons or evil to flourish.

In all of the current affairs programmes on television operating under the political rule of law, it is impossible for supernatural beings as political rulers or political public officials etcetera, to speak intelligibly on any issue or project without it appearing insane because of what they are up against under the real rule of law.

The media is a scientific and social scientific method of providing or disseminating information for the civil scientific constitution. It is meant to be an essential tool for policing under the real rule of law. Unfortunately, the media is being used under the political rule of law to create and maintain lawlessness. It has become an essential aid in the red colonization of the world. It has been converted from the scientific to the supernatural, both direct and indirect supernaturalisms. It is used by demons for acts of terrorism, racist crimes against the vulnerable.

The real rule of law requires supernatural beings to be educated on how to be law abiding as supernatural beings. Common law establishes the way to make the uncivilized civilized, which requires education. You cannot be educated as if you are a constitution or being you are not, a supernatural being cannot be educated as if a civil being and a civil being cannot be educated as if a supernatural being, because the world will be full of educated illiterates.

The real rule of law must be incorporated into every discipline or specialty or subject in education for them to be suitable, in some cases the disciplines or specialities or subjects might be incompatible with the real rule of law and have to be stopped.

Under the real rule of law, the civil scientific constitution, the law lord, is a representation of the amalgamation of the three arms of government, the executive, the legislature, and the judiciary. In the new police service operating under the real rule of law, the law in living form, the civil noble constitution, is the commissioner of supernatural beings as police officers, if they satisfy all the requirements. These commissioned officers will be the enforcers of the law amongst their peers, supernatural beings.

The right to self-determination

The right to self-determination under the political rule of law is defined as the right of people of a state to govern themselves without interference, the right of people to determine their own political status and to be free from alien domination, including the right to construct their own independent state. However, independence is not the only possible outcome of the exercise of the right to self-determination, as is evident in Scotland in the United Kingdom.

This is the political definition of self-determination that does not include supernatural beings; this was developed as if all beings do not have supernatural powers and senses.

What should the right to self-determination be given the existence and nature of the supernatural constitution?

The purpose of the rule of law is for people to live and let live, to eliminate the strong oppressing or dominating the weak by unnecessarily creating hostile living conditions for the strong to survive and for the weak to perish. The purpose of the real rule of law is to eliminate the racist vicious manipulations of the strong to create hostile conditions in order to be worshipped by the weak. The lives, physical and mental wellbeing of the weak are at the mercy of the wicked under the political rule of law. The concept of politics or the political rule of law or the political democratic process is for the strong to dominate the weak.

The purpose of the real rule of law is to eliminate racism or the political rule of law, to introduce individual rights which create the right to self-determination. The political rule of law creates slavery and the real rule of law creates freedom. Propagandists advocating the political rule of law, the political democratic process, including people, supernatural beings, in the decision making process in government appeal to the god complex nature of the supernatural constitution. The political democratic process will give them the opportunity to play or be gods in the lives of others. This is like a drug, a recovering alcoholic whose drink is spiked with alcohol to make the alcoholic regress, to lose self-control by becoming an alcoholic again. The madness will escalate to the point that they start using supernatural powers and senses to effect changes in the lives of the vulnerable, establishing total lawlessness.

The political rule of law has the appeal of giving supernatural beings opportunities to be the ones chosen in the lawlessness created to be the leaders, elevation above their peers, which is rotational. The opportunity to power trip for supernatural beings is more important than law and order. It is astonishing that under the political rule of law, the political democratic process, to exercise the right to vote in an election, represents a loss of the right to self-determination. The exercise of the right to vote is a loss of the right to self-determination.

The political issues in political party manifestoes under the political rule of law are outside the reality of possibilities, insanity, they are issues that have already been decided or mandated within the reality of possibilities under the real rule of law. So, this means that participation in the political rule of law amounts to selling your soul to the devil, for those that can use or afford the currency, barbarism.

The political process requires the compromise or corruption of issues already decided or mandated, the creation of problems, which incorporates death, ageing, illnesses or diseases, inequality, poverty, etcetera, into the lives of people. Supernatural beings whose constitutions are political are the only beings that can of their freewill decide to be part of the political process or reject the political process by upholding the law. Civil beings are naturally legal beings not political and cannot fit into the political process, unless their constitutions are changed like a man becoming a woman or a woman becoming a man, a transsexual.

The political rule of law is a suicide pact made by supernatural beings, and the real rule of law is a cry for help from the vulnerable to be rescued from the self-destructive nature of the supernatural constitution in the form of the right to self-determination.

The law confirms without a doubt that the political rule of law, political parties, political party campaigns, political party conferences, etcetera are breaches of the peace, acts of aggression, crimes against humanity, abominations.

Under the political rule of law, the right to self-determination is being used by wicked supernatural beings to create a different political faction for different lawless purposes because they are being oppressed or dominated by another political faction.

You feel oppressed or dominated or violated if there is no

rule of law. The current political rule of law being applied around the world that is not the real rule of law will continue to create conflicts and cries for secession from geopolitical zones by different political factions around the world until the rule of law is instituted. These cries for secession will continue until they become cries for secession from the planet.

Secession from a country is running away from oppression or domination or persecution. Why should there be the need to secede from a country where the rule of law has been properly instituted, where individual rights are protected or guaranteed?

The devil has been described as a supernatural being, a disruptive and destructive being, similar to the traits or characteristics of supernatural beings around the world. Should supernatural beings have the right to self-determination?

International and domestic legislations do not recognize the supernatural constitution, which implies that the supernatural constitution does not have the right to self-determination. This suggests that the supernatural constitution can only have this sacred right to self-determination through the civil noble constitution as ruler. The submission to the civil noble lord as ruler must not be political, it has to be legal. The supernatural constitution is by nature political and has to behave appropriately, be law abiding, to be legal. The legality of the supernatural constitution can only be achieved through total submission to the civil noble lord as ruler.

The real rule of law creates the necessary level playing field given the differences between the civil and supernatural constitutions that do not suit the wicked.

The problems associated with lawlessness, economic refugees, or political refugees, emigration or immigration, will be eliminated, the unique identity of a people will be preserved.

Under the political rule of law, international and domestic legislations have been very careful to distinguish civil legal beings from supernatural beings. This is in recognition of the vulnerable nature of the civil constitution compared to the supernatural political constitution, confirming that demonism is beyond the civil noble constitution. Money, goods, and services are tainted with demonism; the law launders money, goods, and services for the vulnerable legal person. This is possible under the sacred legal principle the separation of powers, the nobility, and the working class. Supernatural beings are required to provide goods and services for the nobility under this sacred legal principle and the nobility provide governance, the rule of law. The unfortunate unlawful encroachment of supernatural beings on the jurisdiction of the nobility is demonism, the right to self-determination is beyond the civil noble constitution under the political rule of law and as a consequence protected from the effects or consequences of demonism. The sacred separation of powers in law enforcement indicates a type of trade between the civil and supernatural constitutions.

The natural habitat of a fish is water, although other creatures including man use water, they do not use or need it in the same way as a fish. This is the same way that the natural habitat of man, the civil scientific constitution, is with the civil scientific rights as was developed in the science or Garden of Eden for the first man, Lord Adam. The undermining of the natural habitat of man by supernatural beings is a type of unlawful enslavement or captivity of man, which according to common law, the bible, has severe consequences for both the captor and the captive. For the captive the unlawful habitat or conditions are torturous and as a consequence the captor will be condemned to hell as a proportionate punishment for the wicked given the differences between the civil and supernatural constitutions. The maintenance of the natural habitat of man within the military as commander in chief and without as ruler necessitate the civil scientific protocols from the unscientific, the salute or standing at attention, the bowing to a noble person by commoners etcetera.

The concept of economy or economics is the scientific method of delivering goods and services given the uncivilized unscientific nature of the supernatural constitution. This concept has been misapplied with the divisive racist red or market economy, undermining the regulatory purpose of the blue or state economy.

This indicates that privatization is a type of secession from the state by supernatural beings to undermine the regulatory function of the state creating inequality or racism, lawlessness.

Under the real rule of law, election or selection is a simple one off process by supernatural beings to identify or distinguish civil beings as nobles or rulers, which is permanent. This distinction is a simple compulsory distinction similar to the distinction between male and female babies on birth certificates.

Unfortunately, the political rule of law has created variants or red versions of selection or election of rulers, economics or economy, capitalism etcetera, creating inequality and the persecution of civil beings, undermining the right to self-determination of civil beings.

Supernatural beings that exercise their rights to self-determination to choose between the legal and the political, lose their rights to self-determination when they choose the political rather than the legal, regarding the consequences of lawlessness.

Science, although in most cases is unscientific, provides some degree of independence for man from the god complex nature of the supernatural constitution. The independence is in the forms of money, healthcare including exercise or fitness, the police service, the law etcetera. These inadequate scientific provisions are being compromised by supernatural beings not for the better but for the worse to make the vulnerable completely dependent on the poison of the supernatural rather than the freedom of science. These are violations of the right to self-determination of man, the civil noble constitution.

The law, international and domestic legislations including common law, clearly exempts the legal person, the civil constitution, from the political rule of law and the consequence associated with lawlessness. Supernatural beings that try to draw the exempt legal person into their self-destructive role plays are obviously scheming calamity for the vulnerable. This is an attempt to undermine the right to self-determination of man. Man, the civil constitution, lacks the self-determination to be party to lawlessness because of the lack of supernatural powers and senses but has the natural self-determination to establish the rule of law.

The primary objective or purpose of demons commonly referred to as reds is the criminalization and compromise of civil legal beings. The sacredness of the civil being is the vulnerability of the civil being compared to the supernatural being that serves sacred regulatory purposes. This makes the demon similar to paedophiles or child abusers. Paedophiles or child abusers are segregated from other offenders because of the repulsion of other offenders they attract. They are identified and put on a database monitored and not allowed near children and their victims. Unfortunately, demons, the real paedophiles, have managed to convert or corrupt other supernatural beings to become paedophiles, abusers of the vulnerable.

Reds misapply the principle of equality to compromise civil beings. In the bible, the righteous are exempt from punishments, as was the case with Noah, the reds do not bother to distinguish the good from the evil with their application of punishment. The problem is that the real definition of criminal behaviour is not compatible with the ideology of demonism.

The reds or demons seek different ways to carry out their primary objective, by making their actions appear legitimate through the misapplication of the Christian teachings, and through taking what appears to be special interest in their victims through unlawful supernatural methods, stalking. They also try to achieve their primary objective through jokes and games through forced relationships with their victims.

The world is currently under red colonization rendering the United Nations totally ineffective as a police service. This is confirmed by the composition of the Security Council, and the wrong identification, interpretation and application of the law.

Under the red colonization of the planet everything has been orchestrated for supernatural beings to dominate or oppress civil beings, no level playing field. The unlawful manipulations of demons to create the racist impression, the indignation, that the civil noble lord is totally dependent on the charity of supernatural beings. Imagine the abomination, to make demons feel that their prey is beholden to them.

The purpose of the red colonization of the planet is to establish and maintain lawlessness; the effectiveness of the colonization is the corruption of other supernatural beings to undermine the law. In the created lawless world, the law in living form, the civil constitution, is ridiculed, mentally and physically abused rather than revered. The ridicule of the civil constitution is further enhanced by the misuse of the supernatural powers and senses of supernatural beings to alter the physical appearance or shape of the civil constitution.

Unfortunately, supernatural beings while pretending to be civil beings use their supernatural powers and senses to gain advantages over civil beings for better standards of living. The red colonization of the world has created hostile conditions for inequality and racism to flourish.

They use their supernatural powers to give themselves enhancements to their physiques, in some cases the enhancements are aggressive and do not help their already aggressive constitutions. These enhancements were meant for or better on the nonaggressive civil beings, rather the natural physiques of civil beings are supernaturally compromised for ridicule. For example, the size of the penis has no effect on the civil nature of the civil constitution and creates no imbalance between a civil male and a supernatural female, but creates an imbalance between the supernatural male and the supernatural female. This must be the real reason why a big penis is referred to as a blessing; you cannot confer on yourself a blessing.

The aggressive nature of the supernatural constitution makes aggressive behaviour or practice dangerous, similar to a recovering alcoholic and alcohol, there is the tendency for the behaviour to get out of control and become a serious problem for the vulnerable. These aggressive practices include carnivorous practices.

Supernatural beings believe that as a consequence of what they can do with their supernatural powers and senses, the creation of beings and things, they have the right to unrestricted access to their creations. Under the real rule of law the essential component in the creation of beings or things is the rule of law, using the civil scientific constitution as the standard. The right of access must be within the boundaries of the rule of law for civil and supernatural beings.

For supernatural beings the right to self-determination is limited within the boundaries of the rule of law for peace and security.

The right to self-determination, for both civil and supernatural beings, is the establishment of the real rule of law, individualism.

Collectivism

The world is a globe filled with people, a natural globalization, with a lot of dangers that people must be protected from with adequate policing.

The nature of the danger must determine the strategy for policing. The supernatural constitution, although physically within a boundary, extends beyond the boundary with its supernatural powers and senses. The supernatural constitution can be defined as a global constitution. The civil constitution, a legal being protected by law, although physically within a boundary can be affected by events or beings outside the boundary. This extends the rights or authority of the civil constitution beyond the boundary.

The problems affecting the civil constitution are global problems; the scientific strategy for policing must be global making the planet a state.

The bible, common law, international, and domestic legislations confirm that the supernatural constitution is not indigenous to this planet, Earth. This planet was always meant for civil beings. The bible, common law, international, and domestic legislations confirm that the civil scientific constitution has dominion over any other living thing or being on this planet.

The history of the United Kingdom confirms that the military originated from the nobility, used to protect the Kingdom from external or alien forces, and to keep the peace within the Kingdom.

The police service and the military in the United Kingdom are similar in appearance but the police service has a less formal attitude, a casual familiarity, within and without, than the military, which is a mistake because of the alien nature and behaviour of the supernatural constitution.

Common law in the United Kingdom makes a distinction between the state or land lords and supernatural lords. State or land lords are civil beings and supernatural lords are supernatural beings.

The bible, Mark 12:17, Jesus Christ said to give to Caesar what is Caesar's and to give to God what is God's.

The objective of the military as the real police service is to establish and maintain the real rule of law; actually the military is the rule of law.

It is contradictory for the military to be under the control of political masters, it is the objective of the military to eliminate the political, to arrest and punish political masters for rebellion or incitement to rebellion by advocating political variants of the legal manifesto of the real rule of law. The state Earth has been under construction for a long time, the most significant move towards the construction of the state was with the establishment of the United Nations. The failures of the attempts at the construction of the state are linked to the construction of the political state rather than the construction of the legal state. Supernatural beings undermine or underestimate the significance of the indigenes of the planet, civil noble lords.

The natural habitat of the sacred indigenes of the planet, the legal manifesto of the real rule of law, is essential to the construction of the state.

The state is an extension of the civil scientific constitution, the security of the civil scientific constitution, mental and physical, is essential to the constitution of the military. Common law, which includes the bible, international and domestic legislations, require the distinction between civil beings without supernatural powers and senses and supernatural beings with supernatural powers and senses. This creates the enabling conditions to identify crime and criminal behaviour. This confirms the source and causes of crime. This also stops the abomination of the wicked, to blame, directly or indirectly, the innocent naturally righteous civil beings, for the crimes of the wicked political supernatural beings.

It is not easy to be a civil being, especially a civil being surrounded by supernatural beings. The differences between the civil and supernatural constitutions are not medical disabilities but sacred regulatory disabilities. The rights and privileges rulers enjoy are not for show to dominate or oppress as they are being used by supernatural political rulers making them red or demonic but are sacred regulatory disability rights for civil beings. There are other disability rights developed in common law that are disability rights for civil beings in companionships that are being misused by supernatural beings making them red or demonic.

In the bible, since the creation of Lord Adam, supernatural beings are only allowed to identify civil beings as rulers and to have relationships with civil beings as rulers.

The differences between the civil and supernatural

constitutions require different standards for friendships, relationships, associations, etcetera, to establish equality and consent.

The supernatural constitution is stateless, unscientific, making it insane for the stateless constitution to make important determinations regarding important matters of state like security or economy or science, etcetera.

The civil state or the civil scientific constitution is best suited to determine serious state matters like security or economy or science, etcetera, with available resources.

The laws, the bible, common law, international and domestic legislations, have been very careful to exempt civil beings from supernatural political role plays under the insane political rule of law. The civil scientific constitution as a consequence of not having supernatural powers and senses lacks the capacity to form the determination to participate in the political rule of law. The civil scientific constitution is the living doctrine that the real rule of law is built on. Yet, supernatural beings by manipulations of their supernatural powers and senses make sacred civil beings the subjects or pawns in their political role plays under the political rule of law. Supernatural beings alter the physical appearance of the civil scientific constitution as if the civil being is a mascot for the supernatural political party governing under the political rule of law. This is what life is like for the civil being with the insane supernatural being.

Collectivism under the political rule of law is organized barbarism which has been associated with the state concept;

socialism and communism are advocates of the sacrifice of individual rights for social rights. The concept of collectivism under the political rule of law represents the loss of the individual right to self-determination. The failure of the state under the political rule of law is as a consequence of the lack of distinction between the civil and supernatural constitutions, creating the misunderstanding of the state principle or concept. The state under the real rule of law is an extension of the civil constitution that regulates supernatural beings which creates individual rights.

Supernatural beings have taken advantage of the undermining of the state principle under the political rule of law with the red versions of collectivism, socialism, and communism, by seceding from the state through the privatization of natural resources and the creation of independent political states. These actions undermine further the effectiveness of the state to regulate supernatural beings.

It is interesting to note that the barbarisms or lawlessness that constitute social activities for supernatural beings represent a complete loss of individual rights, for example, alterations done to films, music and television programs, converting the scientific to the supernatural.

Social informal interest in civil beings and other life forms supernatural beings consider to be lower life forms will lead to mental and physical abuse, torture, including death for the lower life forms, their eating habits can attest to that.

The Borg, a fictional species in the star trek drama series and films, forcibly transform or alter the constitutions of other species they consider lower life forms to become drones or zombies with a collective consciousness or mind and no type of individuality or individual rights. This is similar to the red or demonic doctrine, the compromise, and criminalization of civil beings to establish and maintain lawlessness. Other supernatural beings are corrupted to opt for supernaturalism, including supernatural methods of establishing relationships, associations, etcetera. They are manipulated into the supernatural rather than the scientific hence the red colonization of the planet.

Imposters, supernatural beings unlawfully pretending to be civil beings and advocating red lifestyles or lifespans, establishing and maintaining hostile living conditions that are not hostile to supernatural beings but extremely hostile to the real civil beings they are pretending to be are violating the civil constitution's sacred right to self-determination.

The nature of the supernatural constitution makes policing nationally insane or unscientific, and policing internationally scientific.

It is natural for beings including animals to seek refuge in any safe part of the planet from war, poverty etcetera.

Governance or policing internationally, the harmonization of laws to create a legal state, will eliminate, inequality, including the elimination of one part of the planet having better living conditions than another part.

There have been instances of problems in a part of the world developing to become international problems, like, diseases, poverty through red economics, democracy or politics, religions, etcetera.   There are a lot of instances where bad practices within a state or nation have developed into international crisis. This suggests that governance or policing has to be international rather than national. This will necessitate the conversion of national governments to branches of an international police service.

It is not the severity of the punishment that deters or reduces crime or criminal behaviour but a truthful identification or definition of crime or criminal behaviour, the establishment of the real rule of law.

The political rule of law is unlawful policing that creates crimes or criminal behaviour.

Author's notes

The right to self-determination is a complex legal principle in international law given the existence of the supernatural being and the differences between the civil legal being without supernatural powers and senses recognized in international law and the supernatural illegal being with supernatural powers and senses not recognized in international law.

The planet is currently under red or demonic colonization, the deliberate unlawful creation of hostile conditions that directly or indirectly persecutes the natural indigenes of the planet earth, civil legal beings without supernatural powers and senses.

The demonic colonization of the planet is responsible for racism or discrimination, inequality, politics, religions, poverty, red economics, the advocacy of the supremacy of supernatural beings over civil beings.

These hostile conditions undermine the prime directive that civil beings are the rulers of this planet and have supremacy over any other living thing or being on this planet, which is a sacred type of equality given the differences between the civil and supernatural constitutions.

The undermining of the sacred determination that civil beings are rulers of this planet and the imposition of hostile conditions responsible for lawlessness, the political rule of law, the red or demonic colonization of the planet are violations of the prime directive, violations of the right to self-determination of civil beings.

The right to self-determination is the establishment of the

rule of law, the upholding of the prime directive, and the fulfilment of the legal manifesto of the rule of law.

The political manifestoes of the political rule of law are alien to this planet, created by supernatural beings that are aliens to this planet.

It is important to note that the bible identifies the civil and supernatural constitutions as able bodied distinct beings.

Author's biography

My name is Lord Loveday Ememe. I was born in the United Kingdom. I am of African origin. I am of a civil noble constitution, without supernatural powers and senses.
I am a graduate of an Anglican seminary school. I graduated from the University of East London with an honours degree in law.

Bibliography

The Bible

Star Trek drama series and films by Gene Roddenberry